Art and Culture

Mardi Gras

Subtraction

Jennifer Prior, Ph.D.

Consultant

Lorrie McConnell, M.A.
Professional Development Specialist TK–12
Moreno Valley USD, CA

Publishing Credits

Rachelle Cracchiolo, M.S.Ed., *Publisher*
Conni Medina, M.A.Ed., *Managing Editor*
Dona Herweck Rice, *Series Developer*
Emily R. Smith, M.A.Ed., *Series Developer*
Diana Kenney, M.A.Ed., NBCT, *Content Director*
June Kikuchi, *Content Director*
Stacy Monsman, M.A., *Editor*
Michelle Jovin, M.A., *Assistant Editor*
Fabiola Sepulveda, *Graphic Designer*

Image Credits: p.5 Flory/iStock; pp.8–9 Photoservice/iStock; p.10 Pictorial Press Ltd/Alamy; p.17 JeffG/Alamy; p.18 Rosa Irene Betancourt/Alamy; p.24 Brian J. Abela/Shutterstock; p.25 Nicole Weaver/Alamy; p.26 Mandoga Media/Alamy; pp.27, 31 Global Pics/iStock; all other images from iStock and/or Shutterstock.

All companies, titles, and products mentioned in this book are registered trademarks of their respective owners or developers and are used in this book strictly for editorial purposes. No commercial claim to their use is made by the authors or the publisher.

This is a work of fiction. Names, characters, businesses, places, events, and incidents are either the products of the author's imagination or used in a fictitious manner. Any resemblance to actual persons, living or dead, or actual events is purely coincidental.

Library of Congress Cataloging-in-Publication Data

Names: Prior, Jennifer Overend, 1963- author.
Title: Art and culture : Mardi Gras / Jennifer Prior.
Description: Huntington Beach, CA : Teacher Created Materials, [2018] | Includes index. |
Identifiers: LCCN 2017049092 (print) | LCCN 2017051507 (ebook) | ISBN 9781480759985 (eBook) | ISBN 9781425857486 (pbk.).
Subjects: LCSH: Carnival--Louisiana--New Orleans--Juvenile literature.
Classification: LCC GT4211.N4 (ebook) | LCC GT4211.N4 P75 2018 (print) | DDC 394.2509763/35--dc23
LC record available at https://lccn.loc.gov/2017049092

Teacher Created Materials

5301 Oceanus Drive
Huntington Beach, CA 92649-1030
http://www.tcmpub.com

ISBN 978-1-4258-5748-6

© 2018 Teacher Created Materials, Inc.
Printed in China
Nordica.022018.CA21701404

Table of Contents

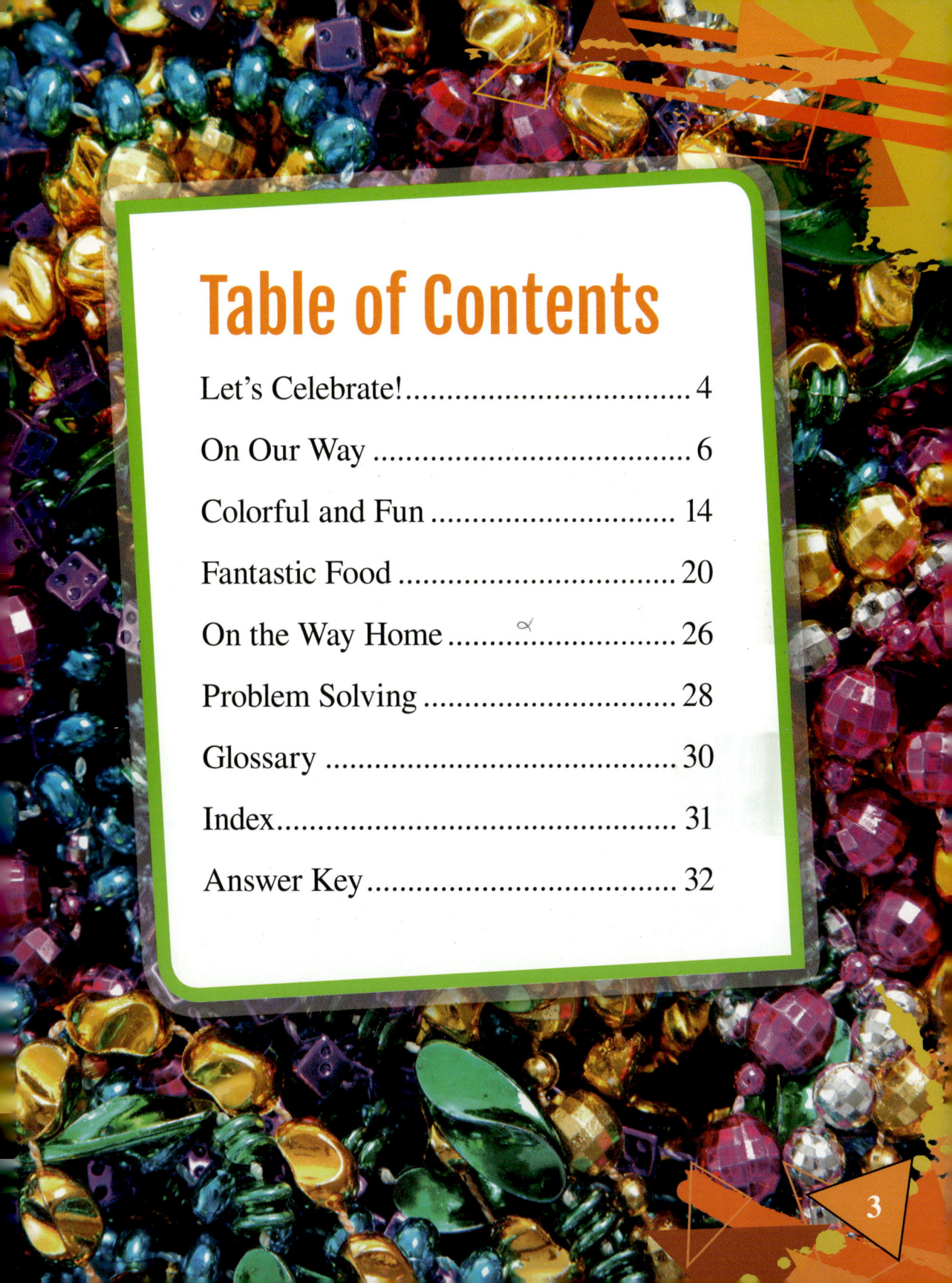

Let's Celebrate! 4
On Our Way 6
Colorful and Fun 14
Fantastic Food 20
On the Way Home 26
Problem Solving 28
Glossary 30
Index 31
Answer Key 32

Let's Celebrate!

I am in a great mood! I am packing for a trip with my family to New Orleans. We are going to Mardi Gras (MAHR-dee GRAH). My dad grew up in New Orleans. He thinks Mardi Gras is the best party in the world!

"Dad," I say as we load the car with our bags. "Can you teach me more about Mardi Gras?"

"Sure!" he says. I sit back and get ready to learn all about this fun **festival**.

Mardi Gras parades feature bright, fun colors.

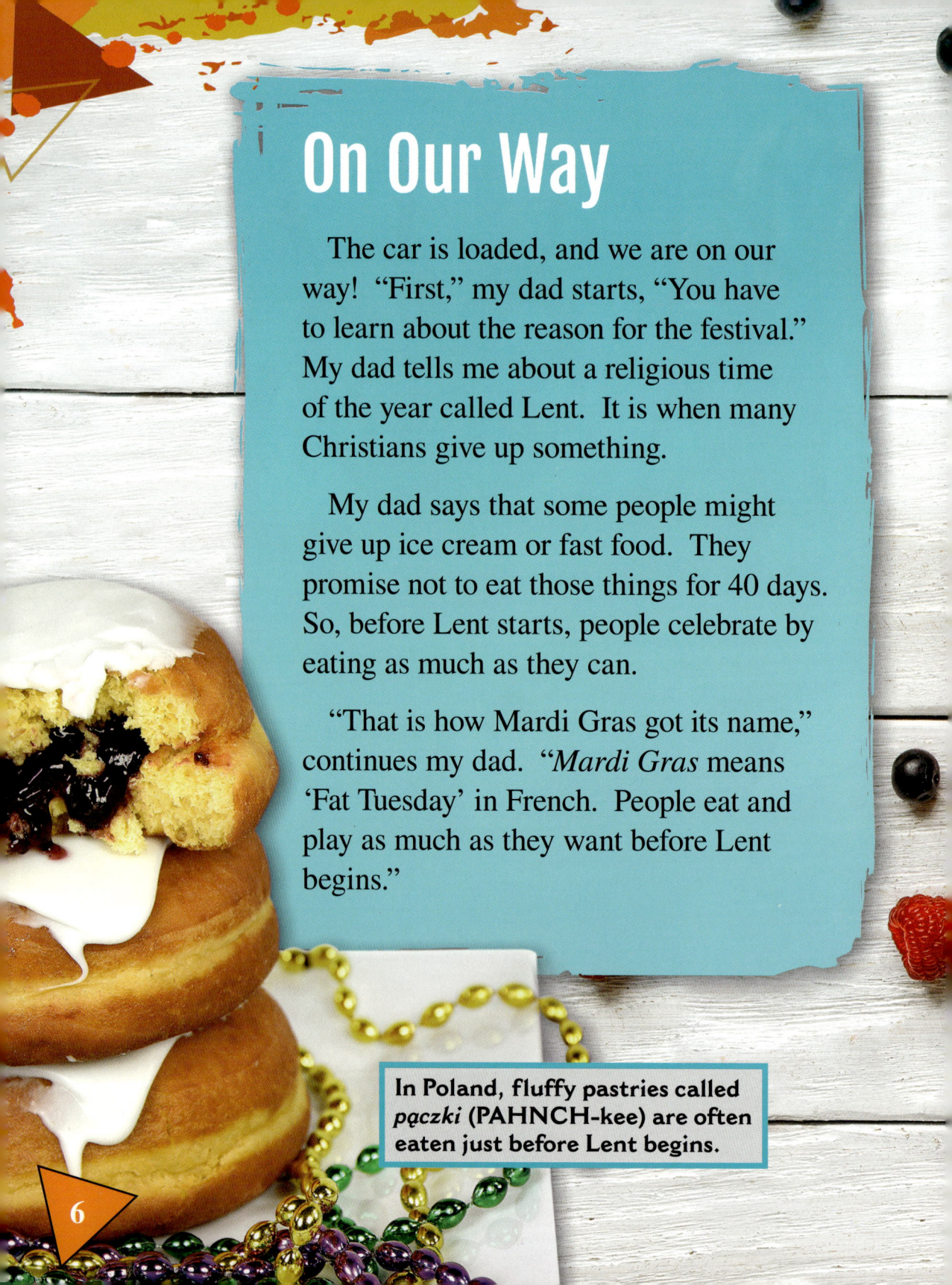

On Our Way

The car is loaded, and we are on our way! "First," my dad starts, "You have to learn about the reason for the festival." My dad tells me about a religious time of the year called Lent. It is when many Christians give up something.

My dad says that some people might give up ice cream or fast food. They promise not to eat those things for 40 days. So, before Lent starts, people celebrate by eating as much as they can.

"That is how Mardi Gras got its name," continues my dad. "*Mardi Gras* means 'Fat Tuesday' in French. People eat and play as much as they want before Lent begins."

In Poland, fluffy pastries called *pączki* (PAHNCH-kee) are often eaten just before Lent begins.

LET'S EXPLORE MATH

I am so excited to get to New Orleans! My mom puts me in charge of keeping track of our location.

1. My mom tells me that we have to travel 98 kilometers. If we drive 42 kilometers before stopping for lunch, how many more kilometers do we still need to travel? Use the part-part-whole model to find the solution.

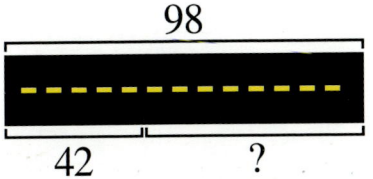

2. Is your answer reasonable? How do you know?

As we pull into New Orleans, I am amazed. The costumes are so bright! And everyone looks like they are having so much fun. I tell my mom that it looks like a carnival is in the streets.

"That is a good name for it," she says. "In the United States, we have Mardi Gras. But people around the world have their own parties. Some people call it Carnival (kar-nee-VAWL). Mardi Gras starts about two months after Christmas. It ends the day before Lent starts."

The French Quarter of New Orleans is famous for its Mardi Gras parties.

As we walk through the streets, I see a stack of brochures. I grab one as I walk by. At the top it reads *Mardi Gras History*. I open it fast, **eager** to know more.

I read that the Mardi Gras festival in New Orleans is the biggest in the country. But it did not start here. It came from Europe. The French came to Louisiana in 1699. Their ships landed on the day before Carnival. So, they had a small party. That was the country's first Mardi Gras. Over the years, it has grown bigger and bigger. Now, it is a huge party!

René-Robert Cavelier was the explorer who landed in Louisiana and said the land belonged to France.

map of France

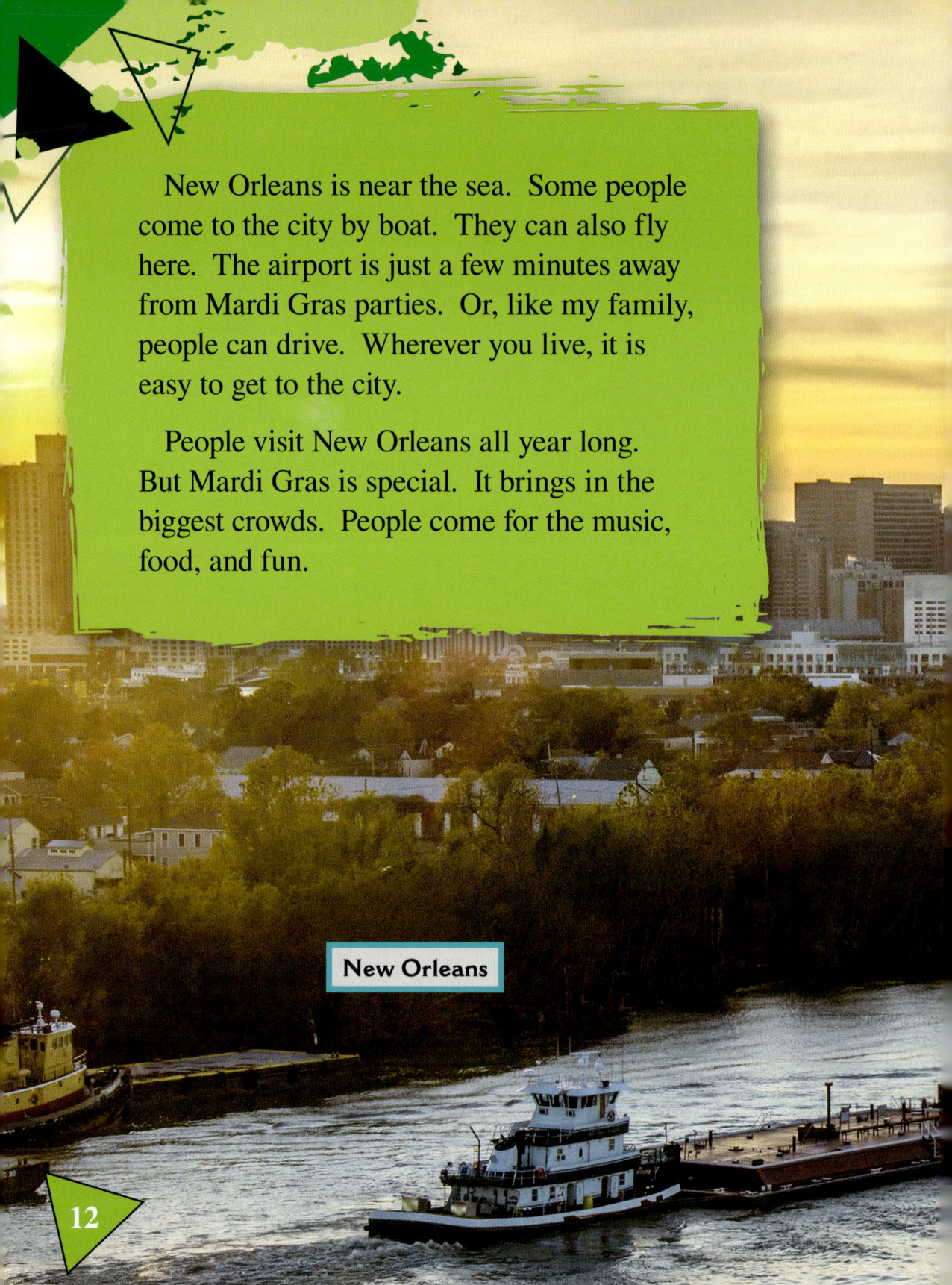

New Orleans is near the sea. Some people come to the city by boat. They can also fly here. The airport is just a few minutes away from Mardi Gras parties. Or, like my family, people can drive. Wherever you live, it is easy to get to the city.

People visit New Orleans all year long. But Mardi Gras is special. It brings in the biggest crowds. People come for the music, food, and fun.

New Orleans

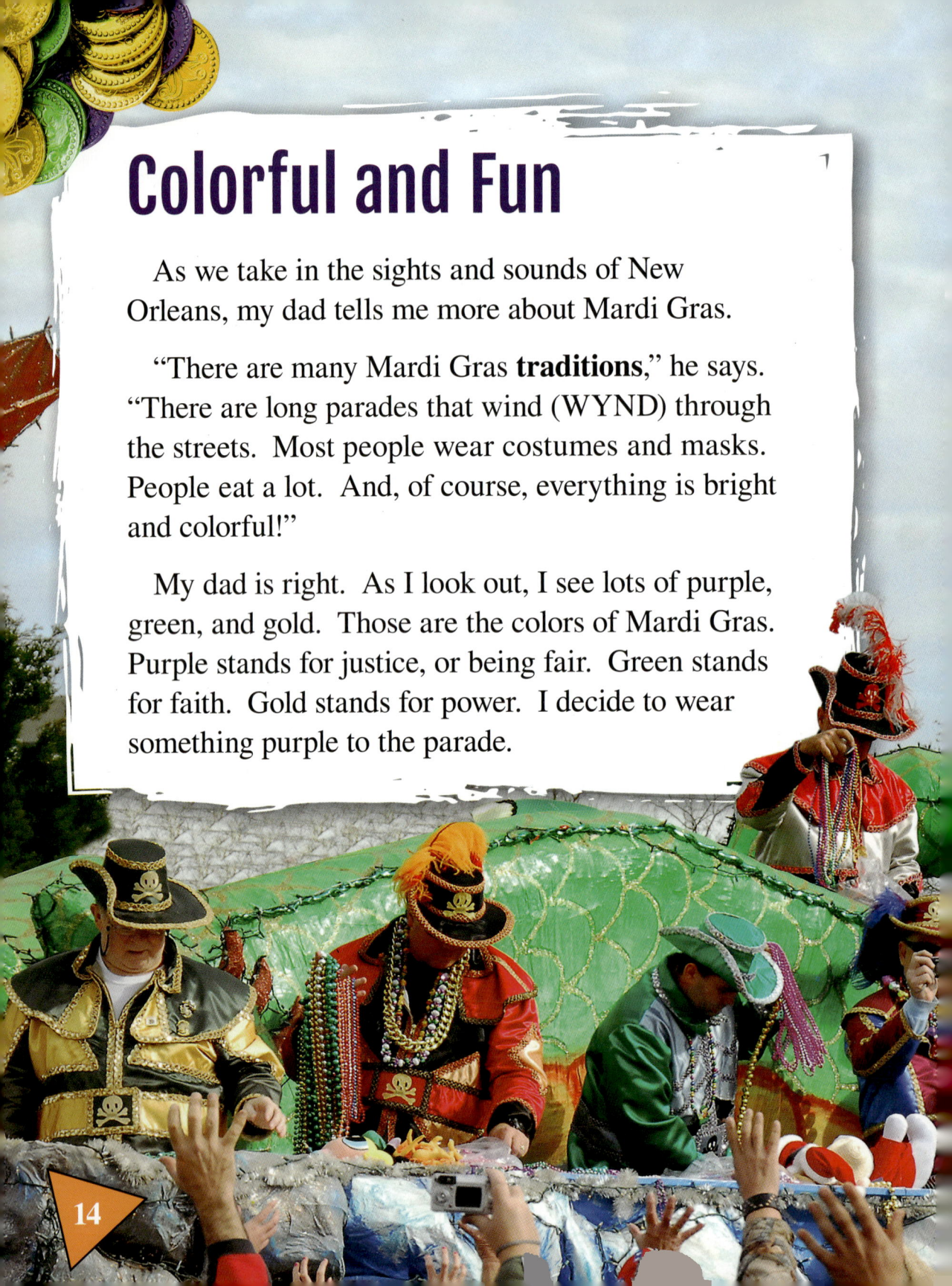

Colorful and Fun

As we take in the sights and sounds of New Orleans, my dad tells me more about Mardi Gras.

"There are many Mardi Gras **traditions**," he says. "There are long parades that wind (WYND) through the streets. Most people wear costumes and masks. People eat a lot. And, of course, everything is bright and colorful!"

My dad is right. As I look out, I see lots of purple, green, and gold. Those are the colors of Mardi Gras. Purple stands for justice, or being fair. Green stands for faith. Gold stands for power. I decide to wear something purple to the parade.

LET'S EXPLORE MATH

While we walk, we go into a store to buy things for the parade. We pick out bright coins and little plastic trinkets, such as necklaces and keychains.

1. I pick out 35 trinkets. My dad gives me some more. Now, I have 57 trinkets. How many trinkets did my dad give to me? Draw an open number line similar to the one below. Use it to find the solution.

2. I pick out 28 coins. I give 7 of the coins to my dad. Then, I give 8 of the coins to my mom. How many coins do I have now?

Mardi Gras parade

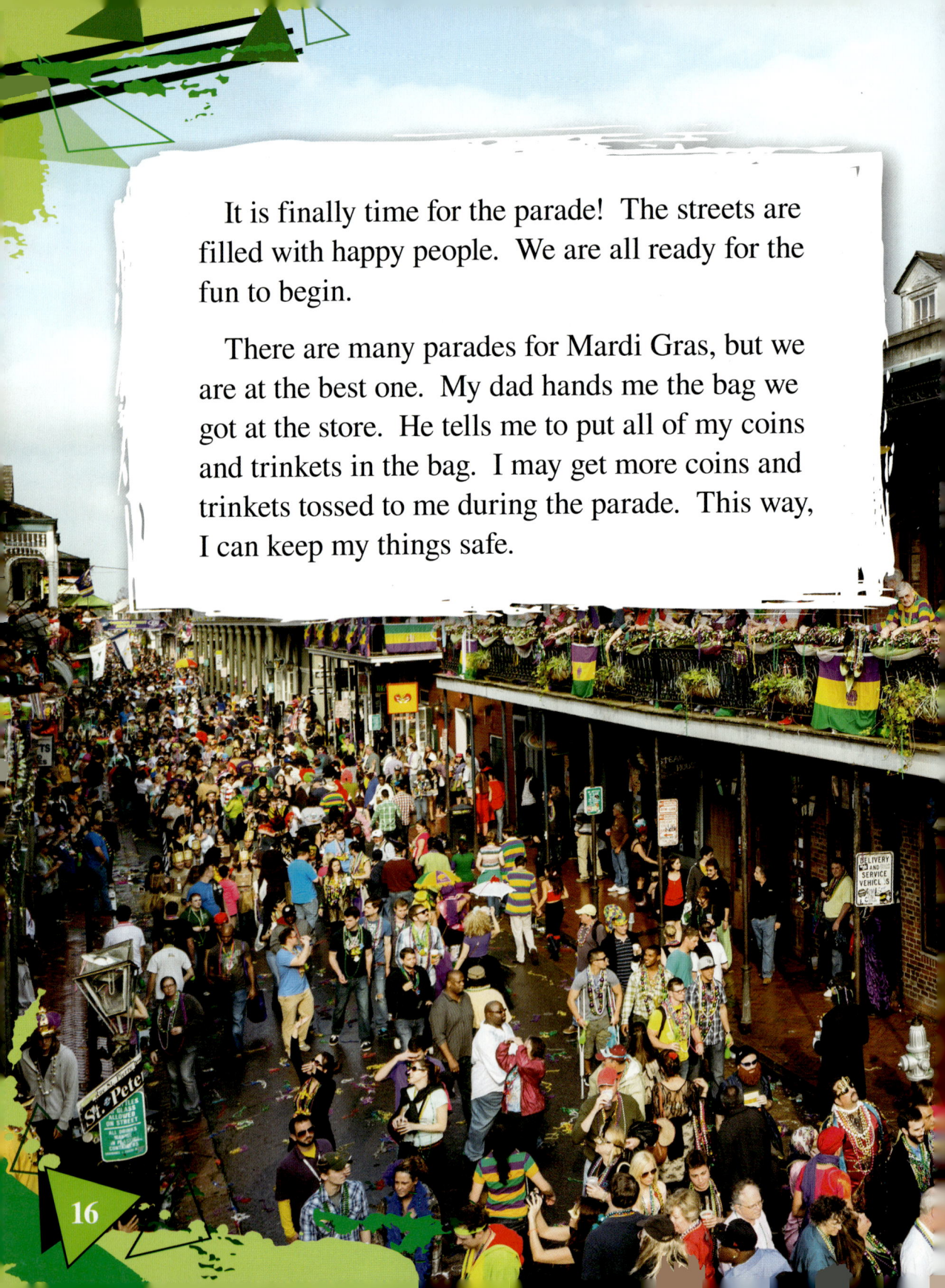

It is finally time for the parade! The streets are filled with happy people. We are all ready for the fun to begin.

There are many parades for Mardi Gras, but we are at the best one. My dad hands me the bag we got at the store. He tells me to put all of my coins and trinkets in the bag. I may get more coins and trinkets tossed to me during the parade. This way, I can keep my things safe.

People wear masks, bright colors, and face paint at Mardi Gras parades.

At the parade, I fit right in with my purple shirt. Then, we go into a mask shop. My mom buys me a purple and green mask. Now, I am really part of the party!

Mardi Gras and masks go together. The tradition began long ago. Back then, people were put into **classes**, or groups, based on how much money they had. People from higher classes did not **interact** with people from lower classes. Masks changed that. They made everyone look the same. Today, masks are just part of the fun.

LET'S EXPLORE MATH

At the mask shop, the clerk tells me there are 64 masks on the wall. My mom counts 42 masks with feathers. How many masks do not have feathers? Use the model to write an equation and find the solution.

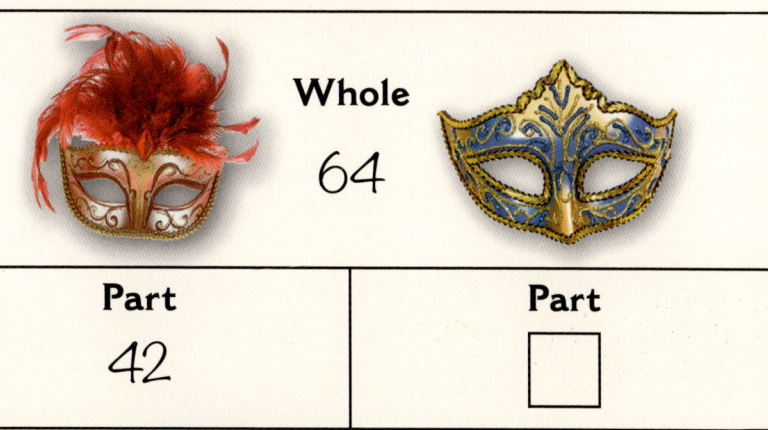

Whole 64	
Part 42	Part ☐

Fantastic Food

After the parade, it is dinnertime. Food is a big part of Mardi Gras. I order crawfish. They are delicious! My mom and dad eat muffuletta (muhf-uh-LET-uh) sandwiches. These round sandwiches are huge! They are a Mardi Gras tradition. For dessert, I want to order beignets (ben-YAYS). But my dad tells me to wait. He has already picked our dessert—a treat called king cake.

muffuletta sandwich

boiled crawfish

King cake is so tasty! The cake has a circle shape, just like a crown. It is covered with purple, green, and gold sugar. The sugar looks like jewels.

The outside of the cake is bright and pretty. But it is what is inside that is truly **unique**. Baked inside each king cake is a plastic baby doll! Whoever gets the baby doll in a slice of cake gets to have the next party.

This slice of king cake has the plastic baby doll.

22

LET'S EXPLORE MATH

After we eat the king cake, my dad orders some beignets for us to try later. The king cake costs $15. The beignets cost $9 less. How much do the king cake and beignets cost altogether? Explain your reasoning using drawings and equations.

beignets

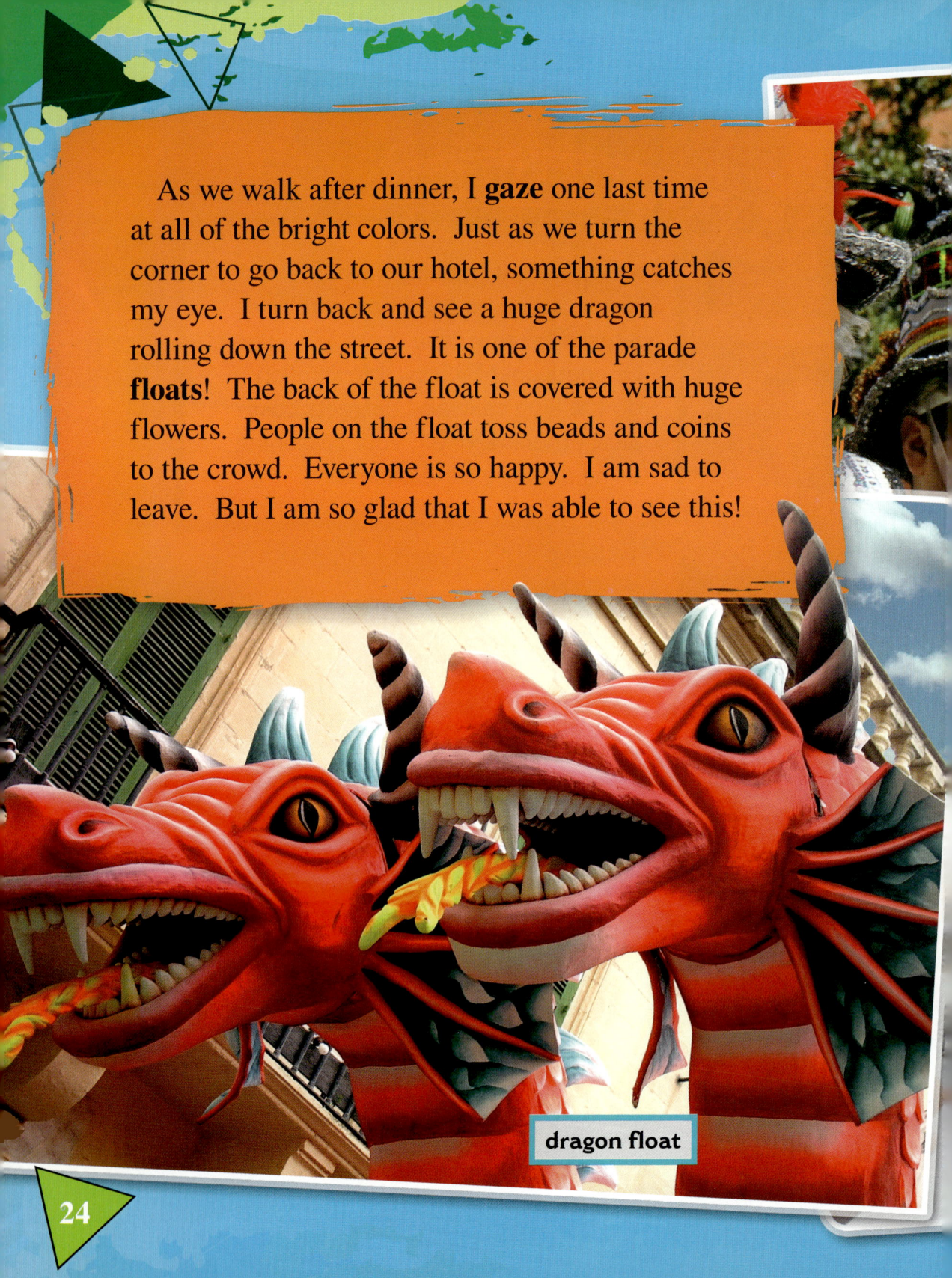

As we walk after dinner, I **gaze** one last time at all of the bright colors. Just as we turn the corner to go back to our hotel, something catches my eye. I turn back and see a huge dragon rolling down the street. It is one of the parade **floats**! The back of the float is covered with huge flowers. People on the float toss beads and coins to the crowd. Everyone is so happy. I am sad to leave. But I am so glad that I was able to see this!

dragon float

Music is a big part of any Mardi Gras celebration.

On the Way Home

After a fun trip, it is time to go home. I wave goodbye to New Orleans as we drive away. On the way home, I tell my mom and dad all that I have learned.

"Did you know that Mardi Gras is a holiday in Brazil?" I ask them. "And people in Denmark and France celebrate it, too."

I spend the rest of the car ride telling my parents fun facts about Mardi Gras. I hope that if I tell them enough, they will take me back next year!

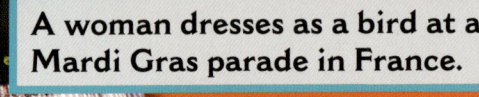

A woman dresses as a bird at a Mardi Gras parade in France.

A woman wears bright colors at a Mardi Gras parade in Brazil.

Problem Solving

Eating crawfish is a big deal in Louisiana. My dad tells us that he used to eat crawfish a lot when he was a kid. So, my mom says we should hold a crawfish-eating contest. We keep track of how many we eat during the entire trip. Answer the questions to find out the results. Use drawings and equations to explain your reasoning.

1. One day at lunch, Mom had 8 crawfish in her bucket. The server put 10 more into the bucket. Mom ate some. Then, there were 6 crawfish in the bucket. How many crawfish did Mom eat at lunch?

2. On the last night of the trip, Dad ate 15 crawfish. He said, "That brings my total to 53!" How many crawfish did Dad eat before this meal?

3. During the entire trip, I ate 38 crawfish. Dad ate 53 crawfish. How many fewer crawfish did I eat than Dad did?

4. I ate 9 more crawfish than Mom. How many crawfish did Mom eat?

Glossary

classes—groups of people in communities who make the same amounts of money

eager—very interested and excited

festival—a special time or event when people come together to celebrate

floats—vehicles that carry things in parades

gaze—look at something in a steady way

interact—talk or do things with others

traditions—ways of thinking, acting, or doing things that have been used by groups of people for a long time

unique—unlike anything else

Index

beignets, 20, 23

Carnival, 8, 10

costumes, 8, 14

crawfish, 20–21, 28

Fat Tuesday, 6

floats, 24

king cake, 20, 22–23

Lent, 6, 8

Louisiana, 10, 28

masks, 14, 17–19

muffuletta sandwiches, 20

New Orleans, 4, 7–10, 12–14, 26

parades, 5, 14–18, 20, 24, 26–27

traditions, 14, 18, 20

Answer Key

Let's Explore Math

page 7:

1. 56 kilometers
2. Answers will vary. Example: *Yes, my answer is reasonable because I know 56 is close to 60 and 42 is close to 40. 60 + 40 = 100, which is close to 98.*

page 15:

1.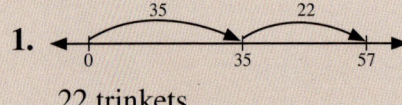

   22 trinkets
2. 13 coins

page 19:

22 masks do not have feathers; 64 (whole) − 42 (part) = 22 (part), or 42 (part) + 22 (part) = 64 (whole)

page 23:

$21; If the king cake costs $15 and the beignets cost $9 less, then the beignets cost $6 because $15 − $9 = $6. So the total of the king cake and the beignets is $15 + $6 = $21. Drawings may include bar models, base 10 blocks, or number lines.

Problem Solving

1. 12 crawfish;
   8 + 10 = 18 crawfish;
   18 − 6 = 12 crawfish
2. 38 crawfish;
   53 − 15 = 38 crawfish
3. 15 crawfish;
   53 − 38 = 15 crawfish
4. 29 crawfish;
   38 − 9 = 29 crawfish